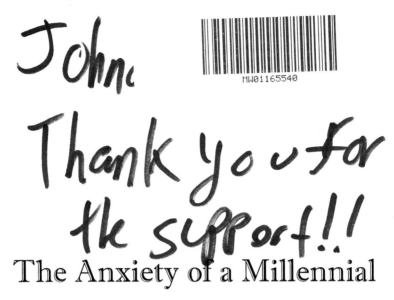

John,

Thank you for the support!!

The Anxiety of a Millennial

A Poetry Compilation

by Samuel M. Mangold-Lenett

Best,
SML

DORRANCE
PUBLISHING CO
EST. 1920
PITTSBURGH, PENNSYLVANIA 15238

Dorrance Publishing Co
585 Alpha Drive
Pittsburgh, PA 15238
Visit our website at www.dorrancebookstore.com

ISBN: 978-1-4809-2561-8
eISBN: 978-1-4809-2331-7

FOREWORD
(November 23, 2015)

By Santa J. Ono, PhD

Rates of depression and anxiety in American college students have risen in the last 10 years, according to reports. One recent study finds that Americans over the age of 30 aren't as likely to identify themselves as "happy" as that age group did in previous decades. Thus evaporates a phenomenon called the "happiness advantage", associated with aging, although one in three adults still identifies as "happy".

Experts speculate that this trend toward downheartedness might be the result of economic insecurities that have arisen since the financial collapse in 2008. It may be the unintended consequences of parents raising sons and daughters to enjoy self-confidence and other advantages the prior generation did not, yet failing to instill the skills needed to face adversity.

Whatever is going on, the worried state of affairs captured the attention of University of Cincinnati student, Samuel Mangold-Lenett, and he decided to write about it. Born and raised in Cincinnati, Mangold-Lenett attended Sycamore High School in suburban Cincinnati and took up writing as a therapeutic endeavor. His efforts took the form of poetry, and the results appear in this volume – his first published collection – titled "The Anxiety of a Millennial." His poems explore millennials' feelings as they come of age and forge their way into the future.

How is the millennials' experience of anxiety different from those in previous generations? Says Mangold-Lenett: "I define 'millennial anxiety' as a feeling of complete connectedness: at any given moment, we are connected to the entire world through the presence and use of 'smart' technology. This is unique because my generation is the only group that has had *gradual* exposure to the presence of this technology in their upbringing. Yes, other demographics had it introduced to them gradually as well, but my generation is the first to have it exposed to us at a young age," he continues.

"We are the last generation – at least the last foreseeable generation – to grow up with *and* without this connectedness. Millennial anxiety is a yearning for nostalgia and legitimate personal connection when the world around you is more focused on reality television and validation from social media. It is wondering what our role in an ever-expanding world is when at the same time we can fit the entire universe in our pockets."

It is certain that the world will hold many more challenges to cause anxiety for all of us, millennials included. Equally undeniable is that facing into those worries is a part of life – it can lead to growth and, oftentimes, a silver lining. Talking about your cares and fears can be a big step toward healing. Those who read this collection, whether you are 20, 30, or 70, may find in its pages some comfort in knowing that you are not alone and that someone else knows how you feel and can empathize. I hope you will not be reluctant to reach out to others to share your worries. Do the same for them and listen when those around you need to be heard. If your anxiety or sadness becomes more long-lasting than temporary, please do not hesitate to contact a counselor or check out the suggestions on the National Alliance on Mental Illness website at http://www.nami.org/Find-Support.

Santa J. Ono is the president of the University of Cincinnati.

Author's Note

You will notice that the following pieces do not have titles. I chose to omit titles because this compilation is meant to capture the anxiety felt by the coming of age of the millennial generation. Many of my millennial peers – myself included – feel as though they are creating their own path without any form of guidance or clue where they are going. By giving my writings titles, I would be giving the audience insight to what they are about to bear witness to – life does not do this, so I will not do this. If it is necessary to refer to specific poems, I would request that each piece be referred to by its first line.

I

I have written song after song and line after line

to try to capture a rhythm that shows me how I work – a pattern

To capture my thoughts on paper and to try and learn about myself,

but all I have picked up on is that the more I learn the less I know

who I am.

II

Life is great –
pine trees and telephone poles,
autumn leaves fall and cigar smoke rises.
Cultural ambiguity breeds patriotism,
and I am the forgotten son
lost at sea.
Stuck between a Catholic rock and a Hasidic hard place
constantly searching for identity and always falling short -
Unable to achieve my own standards for what I hold the world to,
and heartbroken by the Queen of Hearts herself.
A thousand eyes, they gaze into my soul and they tell me –
"You are not good enough,"
And all the while,
I'm a cynic because I'm *sad*?
If anyone understood – if they could –
They would see I have not given up, and I never will.
Life isn't a circle, life is a wheel, always rolling over the hurt, pushing
forward with ambition to find the next greatest mind, but never ap-
preciating what is already here, or at least what was there.
We don't live in the moment, we idealize the past, and I am sorry I
wasn't good enough for you, but I am exceptional for
Me.

III

You are a mountain,

a literal fountain of knowledge;

the last one standing at the final hour -

to all you show power.

Fighting -

every second, every minute –

then, then you die.

Not a noble death that you've dreamed of, not the one fit for a hero,

but a coward's calling.

Out of your arm sticks a needle;

every sin and misdeed done to you, by you, for you.

You bottled up to embody something new.

An image of purity, a beacon of hope,

it's no wonder that under the pressure you finally broke.

Each and every breath drawn pushes you once more -

fixation upon your addiction -

getting twisted becomes your mission.

Out of your corpse will stick a needle;

the shell of one I used to call a friend,

now is dead on a hospital's bed.

A hole is where you will call home,

and I pray that sickness doesn't kick you out

because acceptance and love is what Heaven is all about.

IV

I have a feeling these memories will never fade,
not until the final day,
not until we separate.
I gave and I gave until I had nothing,
and that's when you took the rest.
Not my dignity, nor my pride;
you robbed me of my faith –
in humanity, in tomorrow.

V

I'm not quite sure where to begin.
Like you all, I am full of sin:
betrayal, doubt, and theft, just to name a few.
Once a wise man told me that *love* gets in the way,
Now let's visit his grave and see who is there today.
Who lived life happier: the miser or the scrooge?
When really, we're all indifferent
me, him, and you.
It is not my intention to condemn us all
because we are all the same
but from different points of view.
To many I may seem happy, smiling with glee
but really I'm just an ape, an ape without his tree.
A tree without an ape is a common fact of nature
an ape out of nature is afraid of the world.
My point is quite simple, it really is indeed,
be true to your nature,
don't change yourself for greed.

VI

A cancerous cell, a mutated growth
I fear this has become my image of self
I am secure in who I am, but I cannot find strength
I am confident in what I say, but I have no faith.
Faith is a tricky thing, man goes from fear to adoration,
then back to fear, and then to hatred.

VII

My shadow
My only friend
My companion until the end
This isolation grows every day
My life mission, I'm no longer sure of
My goal is to make it out alive with
My shadow,
Until the end.

VIII

Starry skies light-years away - I wish I could blast off and stay among them.

Jumping and falling, every single day.

Turmoil and struggle - *I found Mars*.

A thought crossed my mind – *cars*.

Why do we have them, why are they needed?

What is the purpose for us being created?

How did we get here?

Where are we going?

How have we made it this far without really knowing?

They call me a dreamer, and push me away.

Labeled a misfit, but I think its okay;

I cannot live a life where I cannot dream.

This life is a tapestry, our existence is the seams.

Look at the colors, watch how they go.

Why was I given this life?

Is there meaning, how so?

Am I forsaken to live a life pointlessly seeking?

I question everything, but find no answers.

Knowledge is a gift;

curiosity, a cancer.

IX

Don't give up on me
I won't give up on you
Don't give up on me
Like how all the others do
Don't give up on me
I'll pull you from the sand
Don't give up on me
I gave to you my hand
Don't give up on me
My questions, you'll never know
Do not give up on me
Cause I'm here to stay
Do not give up on me
I've never looked for the easy way
Do not give up on me
Because I won't give up on you
Please
Don't give up on me
Because I love you

X

"Never give up"
is what I have always been told.
"Never give up". It gets really old.
Beaten and broken and thrown right aside
I never gave up,
I just took bigger strides.
The way you were treated, no one deserves,
and the amount that I love you
no words can describe.
I look down at the ground
with tears in my eyes and pain in my heart, I can only seem to beat
myself up.
I don't know why I feel this way;
so little hope and so much pain,
nothing that's worth fighting for will come with ease,
but it is my life -
and it is my choice -
so this alone is why I will never give up.

XI

All we know is not forever and all we know is love;

when he no longer dances alone with you

and she no longer softly whispers your name,

all we know is loneliness.

All we know is confusion. All we know is pain.

When your friends no longer stand by you, ear-to-ear with wicked

grin

All we know is frustration.

All we know is desperation.

Trying to fix the mess we've made

hour after hour

spent crying for *them*, the people that no longer speak your name.

Clawing your way to the surface just for a glimmer of light -

hoping to *maybe* hear their voice -

This is all I know.

All I know is hope.

If you want, I can share it with you.

XII

The winter's cold will let me know
when my time has come.
The way they run –
thy will be done, on Earth as it is in
heaven.
My search for faith has only shown to what extent to which I know
nothing.

XIII

Fight the good fight
and remember that might does not make right.
It is the compassion in your heart
and the passion in your fist.
It's the impulse in your stomach
with your knowledge and your wits

XIV

I guess I'm just disappointed
in the way things turned out.
Because I loved you, there was never any doubt.
I would have given you – *everything*.
I opened my heart, and I never expected – *anything*.
 To my dismay, you were the one to tear it apart.

XV

The stars align in spectral beauty
washing the universe in black and blue.
Our journey on scale with the rest of existence is miniscule;
stars to molecules,
so what am I to you?

XVI

Fulfill your obligations
Follow through with your words
Never take for granted the clouds and the birds
Be slow to trust, yet easy to love
Be a friend to all and an enemy to none.

XVII

We all think that we are somebody meant for something,
but suffering will take that something and show you just how wonderful
that *nothing* is.

XVIII

Flames that eat and lick the wound -
perpetuating a feeling of impending doom -
with no escape except to jump I will become
a depression in concrete
a massless lump.

XIX

Are we alone?

In a world of constant contact, we are entirely isolated.

I don't understand it,

and maybe I never will.

XX

I woke up
in a sweat,
in a panic,
and in pain.
Why am I here?
Why should I care?
It's as if we're all the same.
I've nowhere to run, nowhere to hide;
I crave to find comfort;
I pray to die.

XXI

Hope is for tomorrow,

to get out of bed and face the world.

I'm not afraid to fight for what I believe in, or die for what I love, but

I am afraid.

I am afraid that if I lose, the world will stop believing and that I will

lose *you*.

XXII

In and out
bustle and hustle
the rap*idity of modernity* makes it obvious how little we appreciate
today.
I am waiting for a table, so that I may scarf down fast food
and then complain about how brief
my youth is.

XXIII

I've had so many mood swings, I swear I've gone insane.
The way they all talk about me, it's like hornets in my brain.

XXIV

A constant search for identity will leave you more certain of what you
believe in,
but completely lost in an effort to find who you truly are.

XXV

I oftentimes find myself at a loss for ways to create the masterpieces
that I find in my mind;
they're so explicit and vivid, yet impossible to reach.
While the madness approaches I can see more clearly,
but my body fails to create.
The vessel for my soul is a flesh cage imprisoning a song bird.
While the flesh rots away, the bird slowly suffocates and dies.

XXVI

The problem with "freedom" is that everyone is so afraid of losing it that they don't appreciate it.

They're so obsessed with maintenance and order that they can't see they've forsaken freedom long ago and are now slaves to the system enslaved by the very freedom they obsess over – that they worship.

XXVII

Time is a virus for which there is no cure except death,

but patience can combat the symptoms.

Patience can make the slippage of time feel merry.

The AZT of Secondhand Syndrome – allowing ignorance to bloom

in place of consciousness -

each hour is a week, but that doesn't stop us from not living in the

moment.

We are all afraid to commit to today, but not afraid enough to look to

tomorrow for salvation.

XXVIII

There is beauty in ambiguity,
and in a world inhabited by parrots,
I am a vulture
waiting for them to pick off the weak so that I may feed.

XXIX

I was born into a time of trial.
Every nation is afraid, and the embodiment of
righteousness
is now a symbol for
entitlement.

XXX

I plunged a knife and into my lungs flowed death.
I saw you there,
where tombstones lined the roads,
I put them there.
The corpses' whispers are screeches to me,
louder and louder and louder and louder
I bathed in their screams,
and I put them there.
The corpses – my friends – animal snippets,
raw, emotion, dead is devotion
the tar that I will boil in for how I live sends a stabbing
sensation
along the road, lined with tombstones,
I make my home.

XXXI

The stars:
whimsical playthings we made for ourselves –
when I close my eyes, I feel close to you but I know
we won't end up in the same place.
The embodiment of kindness, a beautiful soul
a shell of a man, haunted by his sins.
If I hang myself,
can I hold you one last time?
As the setting sun is pure,
beautiful and inspiring of awe,
my actions present me with one fatal flaw:
I loved someone much better than I.

XXXII

Every single moment that we are alive, significant or not, makes us
who we are.

Potential that shines brighter and brighter,

it burns wonder and awe into my retinas.

If only the starlight of humanity burned a little brighter, then maybe
we could cast aside our

vanity,

and rediscover what it means to be kind, acknowledge our mistakes,
and relish in our flaws.

We might appreciate each other more and not fuss over legislature.

I believe that our light is still lit,

and where many of my peers do not care, I still very much give a shit

I know compassion lives on;

It's just hidden,

by fear.

We fear tomorrow, we fear ourselves

The answers can't always be found in leatherbound philosophies col-
lecting dust on shelves, as a collective, we need to shelve that mental-
ity and exploit the broken system's frailty and become its fatality.

If reality is what we perceive to be true, take what God gave you and
perceive a reality where you feel malice towards none and charity to-
wards all.

XXXIII

I overlook the fact that I cannot sleep
due to the way my thoughts dance in my head
I have never seen such a beautiful array of colors
in my life

They dance from corner to corner, wall to wall
all the while I am conscious of it all
seeds of betrayal, initial deceit
the grotesquely bloody, sweaty sheets
the pallet that is my mind
oftentimes goes without
convincing me of sanity, as time will wind
down to a matter of seconds all we know is *doubt*

XXXIV

Line after line, red, rising sun -

hoping my work will be over when the day is done.

Every line represents a fear,

an anxiety or grievance.

The ringing bells begin to convince me

that I have no definition;

I fear that these lines will define me -

not my vision.

these lines hold those who wait -

the most soothing way to release my self-hate.

Tearing and ripping up old lands created by my forefathers with their

Own hands.

I know that life means

something more

but what exactly,

I am not sure.

XXXV

The constant ticking noise
both hands are raised
controlling our destinies
and in a way determining our fates
the verbosity of routine
breeds a sempiternal circular path
like clockwork

XXXVI

Stars at night
are not what they appear to be
light from far way
is what we really see.
A warming kindness
from far away
we welcome it,
and invite them to stay -
to light up our world,
and protect us from harm.
Just barely out of reach
of an awe-stricken child's arm

XXXVII

I'm searching for God.

Am I really, or am I searching for myself?

To find a voice, two flat feet to stand up and testify, to defy, to

redefine my life.

I've turned the other cheek to be spat upon the other;

it's hard to trust an ambiguous God when I can't even trust my neigh-

bors to bring in my

trash cans while I'm away.

So why, in a God, should I let my faith remain?

XXXVIII

Torn out pages, totaled cars
we embody our frustrations
I feel it more than most I guess, and
if what you say is true –
I embody my frustrations,
and that is why I look like you.

XXXIX

Does anyone out there know what this feels like?

To feel so desperate and alone

to be forsaken, by yourself

and then die upon your throne

to wander every day and every night

with no idea where to go

until you fall asleep and collapse on your new, concrete-pavement home?

XL

Humanity is on a ship
headed for nothing short of our own deaths
brought upon ourselves
during our final
breathes

XLI

Lions, tigers, and bears - Oh my
twinkle, twinkle, little star, way up in the sky
where a child reaches and a blue jay flies
up above the world so high
never running late and never on time
a voyage, an adventure
no worries of expenditure
it seems to me that the "real world" is not so real.
Reality is what I make of it -
I refuse to grow old,
I refuse to give a shit.

XLII

Scars –

my body is covered in scars,

from people I loved, from those whom I hated.

No one knows just how many there are, but I guess that's why I am scarred.

Not because people hurt me but because I let it out

in the form of blood,

because

I love the pain.

XLIII

I'm just another in the line.
A worker ant cannot defy his commands,
so I cannot
I must continue to oblige this world filled with lies.
Love is dead;
broken is my heart.
This reality continually tears me apart
into nothingness
just as they say it should be.

XLIV

Is there meaning in this life, or are we just drifting
along
aimlessly?
As time passes and opportunities fly by,
doors are shut and windows are
opened.
But life isn't about those doors that have been shut –
no, life is about taking the
windows -
taking that opening
and blasting it to kingdom come.
Forget what life gives you,
you control your fate.
Not life, not God, but
man.

XLV

I am stuck
somewhere in-between
cold pizza at 3A.M.
and forgetting who I am

When night time hours are spent
thinking of past lovers,
I tend to question my existence
and place in this world

But I am there –
the stone unturned
the playground in Chernobyl –
forgotten.

XLVI

I'm afraid they'll find
my heroin –
what makes me whole inside
and they'll take it all away from me.
They'll take away my pride –
my red-haired, gorgeous heroine
they'll take her away.
One last line and then I swear I'm done,
my heroin saved the day.

XLVII

The stale scent of cigarette smoke and spilled beer out on the patio-
it makes me wonder why we wonder at all.
Knowing brings empowerment, but curiosity fosters pain.
It's a cancer infesting the minds of the sane.

XLVIII

Time flies like the blink of an eye,
here of a second only to say,
"Goodbye."
Cherish every tear drop, treasure every smile,
and maybe time will slow down for
awhile.

XLIX

Don't worry about forever,
focus on today
and live to see tomorrow
forever will find her way.

L

Coffee mug full of whiskey
while he sits at the counter of the diner he's always eaten in since he
was a boy,
he and his friends, lovers, and associates have always eaten here.
Here he has memories,
and the whiskey brings it back.
The whiskey reminds him of a simpler time
where the pain wasn't painful.
It restores the memories of a young man
finding his way through life.

LI

I can't sleep at night,

I'm not asking you to understand but place yourself in my shoes.

It's hard enough to get out of bed,

but for some reason it's a struggle for me to even be alive.

When I wake up the first thing I want to do is slit my throat,

and then I remember that

my life is great –

not because of privilege or opportunity

but because it's life,

it's mine and –

I've made it this far.

CPSIA information can be obtained
at www.ICGtesting.com
Printed in the USA
LVOW10s1454130917
548601LV00017B/284/P